The Battle on the Ice: The History and Legacy of the Slavs' Decisive Victory Against the Teutonic Knights

By Charles River Editors

A medieval depiction of the battle

About Charles River Editors

Charles River Editors is a boutique digital publishing company, specializing in bringing history back to life with educational and engaging books on a wide range of topics. Keep up to date with our new and free offerings with this 5 second sign up on our weekly mailing list, and visit Our Kindle Author Page to see other recently published Kindle titles.

We make these books for you and always want to know our readers' opinions, so we encourage you to leave reviews and look forward to publishing new and exciting titles each week.

Introduction

A Soviet stamp commemorating the 750th anniversary of the battle

"He was taller than others and his voice reached the people as a trumpet, and his face was like the face of Joseph, whom the Egyptian Pharaoh placed as next to the king after him of Egypt. His power was a part of the power of Samson and God gave him the wisdom of Solomon ... this Prince Alexander: he used to defeat but was never defeated…" – *The Second Pskovian Chronicle*

In 1938, the Soviet Union film company Mosfilm released the motion picture *Alexander Nevsky*, directed by Sergei Eisenstein. It is a historical drama depicting the defense of the Republic of Novgorod against an invasion of the Teutonic Knights in the mid-13th century. The eponymous hero of the story, the Prince of Novgorod, leads his troops against the German knights on a field of solid ice. During the battle, called the Battle on the Ice or the Battle of Lake Peipus, the ice breaks and many of the knights drown in the freezing waters, but Nevsky is victorious and the pernicious Germans are vanquished forever.

Far from an attempt to portray historical events, *Alexander Nevsky* is a Stalinist propaganda piece in which the Russian people defy and halt the eastward expansion of the German menace. It is an obvious allegory of the Soviet Union defying Nazi Germany at a time when Soviet-German relations were at their most acrid before World War II. The clothing of the Teutonic warriors inaccurately display swastikas,[1] and the famous scene where they are swallowed up by the ice is also a Stalinist embellishment.[2]

Of course, Soviet Russia was not the first to use the historical conflict between the German West and the Slavic East for propaganda purposes. The German defeat of Russia at the Battle of Tannenberg in 1914 was

---

[1] Alex von Tunzelmann (October 8, 2009) "Alexander Nevsky: Stalinist propaganda in the 13th century," *The Guardian* https://www.theguardian.com/film/2009/oct/08/alexander-nevsky-reel-history.

[2] Donald Ostrowski, "Alexander Nevskii's 'Battle on the Ice': The Creation of a Legend," *Russian History/Histoire Russe*, 33 (2006) pp.289–312.

portrayed as revenge for the Battle of Grunwald in 1410, when the Poles and Lithuanians overwhelmed the flower of the German nobility.[3] The Nazis' vision of *Lebensraum* ("living space") would be conceived as a continuation of Germany's historical destiny to push eastward.[4] The clash forms part of a historical narrative stretching back to the 11th century, when ethnic Germans of the Holy Roman Empire began settling in the Slavic lands along their eastern borders.

That these lands were pagan legitimized colonization in the eyes of the Christians, but the expansion or *Ostsiedlung* ("east settling") assumed a more aggressive character when the papal proclamation of the crusade against the Saracens in 1095 canonized the concept of holy war. In the year 1147, while Christian knights were fighting the Muslims in the Near East as part of the Second Crusade, the German princes to the north were pressing the pope for a crusade against the pagan Slavs and Balts. Pope Eugene III obliged by publishing the bull (decree) *Divina dispenatione*, which declared, "Certain of you, however, (are) desirous of participating in so holy a work and reward and plan to go against the Slavs and other pagans living towards the North and to subject them, with the Lord's assistance, to the Christian religion. We

---

[3] Burleigh, Michael (June 1985), "The German Knight: Making of A Modern Myth," *History Today*, **6** (35), p.27.
[4] Johnson, Lonnie (1996), *Central Europe: Enemies, Neighbors, Friends*, Oxford University Press, p.44.

give heed to the devotion of these men, and to all those who have not accepted the cross for going to Jerusalem and who have decided to go against the Slavs and to remain in the spirit of devotion on that expedition, as it is prescribed, we grant that same remission of sin...and the same temporal privileges as to the crusaders to Jerusalem."[5]

This northern Crusade, also known as the Wendish Crusade, was directed against the Wends, a group of Slavic tribes inhabiting what is now northeastern Germany and northwestern Poland. Their lands bordered the Baltic and thus enjoyed a milder climate than much of the German north. They were rich in resources, in particular furs and fish. Militarily the Germans prevailed, but they only partially succeeded in converting the pagans. Indeed, the crusaders made "no mention of Christianity, but only of money," according to the contemporary Saxon historian Helmold of Bosau.[6]

Nevertheless, the wars against the heathens to the east were renewed in earnest in the 13th century, and it was taken up by two religious orders: the Order of Brothers of the German House of Saint Mary in Jerusalem, more commonly known as the Teutonic Knights, and the Livonian Brothers of the Sword. These were two of the

---

[5] Giles Constable, 'The Second Crusade as seen by Contemporaries,' *Traditio* Vol. 9 (1953), p.255.
[6] Barraclough, Geoffrey (1984). *The Origins of Modern Germany*. New York: W. W. Norton & Company. p.263.

many military orders that arose from the crusades. Their members were knights who lived in community and took the monastic vows of poverty, chastity and obedience and pledged their swords to the defense of pilgrims and the sick. They were usually recruited from the lesser German nobility or from the younger sons of the great houses. Like other military orders, they had been founded in the Holy Land "to avenge the dishonoring of God and His Cross and to fight so that the Holy Land, which the infidels subjected to their rule, shall belong to the Christians,"[7] but they also possessed properties in Europe. In 1226 Duke Conrad I of Masovia (Central Poland) appealed to the Teutonic Order to rescue his domain from marauding Prussians and the Knights obliged by subjecting Prussia to a ruthless campaign of conquest and extermination.[8] The Brothers of the Sword were founded by the Prince-Archbishop of Riga for the purposes of converting the heathen tribes of Livland and Esthland (Estonia). The pope was keen to give his blessing to these ventures and offered privileges, including the remission of sin, for those willing to take up the sword for Christ and his Church.

The prospect of new lands to conquer inspired many Germans, and the words of Pope Urban II when he first called Christians to arms to conquer Jerusalem in 1095

---

[7] *Rules and Statutes of the Teutonic Order* http://www.imperialteutonicorder.com/id186.html.
[8] P. Dollinger (1999) *The Herman Hansa*, Routledge p.34.

might indeed have been addressed to the hungry aristocracy of the Holy Roman Empire: "[T]his land which you inhabit, shut in on all sides by the seas and surrounded by the mountain peaks, is too narrow for your large population; nor does it abound in wealth; and it furnishes scarcely food enough for its cultivators. Hence it is that you murder one another, that you wage war, and that frequently you perish by mutual wounds. Let therefore hatred depart from among you, let your quarrels end, let wars cease, and let all dissensions and controversies slumber. Enter upon the road to the Holy Sepulchre; wrest that land from the wicked race, and subject it to yourselves ... God has conferred upon you above all nations great glory in arms. Accordingly undertake this journey for the remission of your sins, with the assurance of the imperishable glory of the Kingdom of Heaven."[9]

The Teutonic Knights began the invasion of Prussia in 1230, but it was not completed until 1274. Meanwhile the Brothers of the Sword launched an invasion from Riga and by 1260 had conquered the lands roughly corresponding to modern Estonia and Latvia. The power of the military orders eventually reached from the Vistula to Lake Preipus, yet this vast extension of power came at a price because their resources were overstretched: The

---

[9] Robert the Monk's account of Urban's speech, <u>Urban II: Speech at Council of Clermont, 1095, Five versions of the Speech</u> (available as part of the <u>Internet Medieval Sourcebook</u>).

Teutonic Knights were frequently at odds with the Catholic Kingdom of Poland to their south and with other Christian powers such as Denmark. Moreover, the Teutonic and Livonian Orders were military orders, born of the crusading movement, and warfare was their *raison d'être*. At the same time, however, these knights were forbidden to marry or to possess land, meaning that the orders depended on constant recruitment from the German nobility. Land (which could be enjoyed if not possessed), wealth, and status tended to be the attraction rather than the call to knightly honor. While there remained land to conquer, there would be new recruits, but the pope would only give them mandates to invade pagan lands.

The Orders saw two avenues of expansion. The first was southwards into Lithuania, but the Lithuanians resisted by organizing themselves into a strong state. Though warfare with Lithuania was generally continuous throughout the 13th century, the knights could not make serious inroads into its territory. The second possibility of expansion was into the lands of the Rus beyond Lake Preipus. The Rus (from which the name Russia comes) ruled a vast expanse from the Baltic to the Black Seas, though it was already severely weakened when Mongols invaded from the east in 1237. All of the princes of the Rus were forced to submit to the Great Khan or the Golden Horde, a tribal union of Mongols and Turkic peoples inhabiting the southern steppes. The exception was the Prince of Novgorod, who spared his lands the devastation visited upon the other principalities by submitting to the Golden Horde. Consequently, the enormous lands of Novgorod, extending across the Baltic region to Archangelsk on the White Sea, were left unscathed and prosperous. The city of Novgorod itself lay on the Volkhov River just downstream from Lake Ilmen. Known as "Novgorod the Great" (Veliky Novgorod), it was one of the most important cities of Russia, commanding the trade route from the Baltic to the Black Seas.

The principality of Novgorod was Christian, as all of Russia was, but as far as the Teutonic Knights were concerned, its inhabitants were not true Christians. Instead, they were adherents of a sect based in Greek Constantinople which had repudiated the authority of the pope and separated from Western Christianity. To the West, the Christians of Russia adhered to Constantinople and were thus errant brethren. To the Teutonic Knights, the lands of the Rus were the lands of schismatics and thus fair targets for religious war.

This would bring about one of Eastern Europe's most famous battles, fought between the Teutonic/Livonian Knights and the Principality of Novgorod. German knights, having dominated the lands of the heathen Prussians and Balts, wished to command the Eastern

Baltic, and Novgorod stood in the way of this ambition.

The Battle on the Ice: The History and Legacy of the Slavs' Decisive Victory Against the Teutonic Knights examines the events that led to the battle, and what happened on the lake. Along with pictures depicting important people, places, and events, you will learn about the Battle on the Ice like never before.

The Slavs and the Novgorod Republic

The "Viking Rus," as they are sometimes known, were a Scandinavian tribe that historians believe originated in the central coastal area of modern Sweden. As with other Vikings, they set up trade routes around Europe, including the seas and waterways and stretching into Eurasia, dealing in furs, precious metals, and even slaves. What was particularly significant about the Vikings, including the Rus, was their ability and desire to set up colonies. The Vikings found success in the period after the fall of the Roman Empire, an era lasting centuries in which Europe descended into war and barbarity.[10] The Romans might have subjugated the continent, but they also made strides in terms of learning, science, literature, and so on. The Vikings, perhaps in a more circular fashion, also moved the people of Europe and Eurasia forward developmentally. This can be seen in the transformation of the Rus from marauders to settlers, and eventually the standard-bearers of a new version of Christianity. Establishing a network of settlements, first through raids and then through trading, the Vikings' influence stretched far and wide across the continent. They were also known as feared, brutal warriors.

Along with their military prowess and skill at navigating the seas through their advanced ships, the Vikings also

---

[10] Marr 2012

assimilated into local populations through marriage and by taking on the beliefs, languages, and customs of the individual regions in which they settled. The Scandinavian Vikings controlled the forests in the north of the region but failed to take full control of the steppe to the south. The Scandinavians were known as the Rus by the locals, and they started converting to the Byzantine version of Christianity from the influence of southern Greeks. Rus leaders took on Slavic names and intermarried with the local Slav population.[11]

By the mid-9th century, the Rus lived on land to the north of modern Ukraine, in what is now Belarus. Kiev was taken from the Khazars by the Varangian (a synonym for Vikings) Army, led by Prince Oleg in 882, thus beginning the Kievan Rus reign.

The Rus then came into conflict with other powers in the region, including the Byzantines and Khazars. A number of peace treaties were signed, and an area began to form, including Ukraine. The territory dominated by the Kievan Rus included modern-day Ukraine, Belarus, parts of Russia, and stretched all the way up to Finland. Lasting until the middle of the 13th century, at its peak the Kievan Rus spanned the land from the White Sea in the north to the Black Sea in the south. Established as a relatively loose configuration, perhaps best thought of as a

---

[11] Snyder 2016

federation of authorities and people, the Kievan Rus based itself in Kiev and included the town of Novgorod.

Some historians have contested this version of the Rus' origins, with some believing they were descendants of the Slavic tribes and those believing they migrated from Scandinavia. The more conventional narrative describes Scandinavian Vikings settling in Kiev and the surrounding region and adopting the Slavic customs and language, all while integrating into the local population. In any case, it seems clear that Prince Oleg had assumed control of Kiev by 882 and used the city as the base for the Kievan Rus. With this conquest, the Scandinavians essentially controlled river trade routes from the Baltic to the Black Sea and beyond.[12]

The Rus established and controlled trade routes for commodities important to the era. Their control of the River Dnieper around Kiev and beyond was crucial in this trade network. Oleg negotiated with the city at Constantinople, the end of the gateway to global trading routes, over an agreement on trade. The result allowed the Kievan Rus to enrich themselves and develop Kiev as a major city.[13]

Once they established themselves in the region, the Kievan Rus were pitted against the Khazars, who attacked

---

[12] Marr 2012
[13] Marr 2012

the Rus around Novgorod from the east. By then, the Rus already had a reputation for military prowess that was further extended under Grand Prince Sviatoslav I, who ruled in the mid-10th century until 972. Sviatoslav was enthusiastic in his desire to expand the Rus' territory, pushing south into modern Romania and the Balkans, as well as the Volga Valley. Sviatoslav even moved the Kievan Rus capital from Kiev to Pereyaslavets on the Danube River (in today's Romania) in 969.

By the end of his life, Sviatoslav had expanded the Rus' borders down to the Black Sea in the south, the Caucasus in the southeast, and far into Khazar territory in the east. This was much larger than the size of today's Ukraine and demonstrated the Rus' ambition and ability.

Sviatoslav was a pagan, but his successor, Vladimir, adopted Christianity, a crucial element to the development of the region. The story of Vladimir the Great, who was born around 958, is central to the history of the region, and it is a quintessential story of medieval conquest, intrigue, betrayal, and power. Sviatoslav moved to Pereyaslavets and made Vladimir Prince of Novgorod. Vladimir was, however, Sviatoslav's illegitimate son, and his mother was the grand prince's housekeeper, Malusha. Sviatoslav's son from his marriage was Yaropolk, who had been made prince of Kiev, a more prestigious city. After Sviatoslav's death in 972 CE, a civil war broke out between the allies of the three brothers, with Yaropolk based in Kiev, his younger brother Oleg based to the west of the country, and Vladimir in Novgorod. Vladimir was forced to flee to Norway, where he recruited fighters to mount a challenge to Yaropolk's rule. Vladimir's campaign culminated in 978, when he took Kiev, killed Yaropolk, and declared himself prince, using the title, *knyaz*, of all of Kievan Rus.

A coin depicting Vladimir

Vladimir continued in much the same manner as his father, Sviatoslav, for the first years of his rule, expanding territory into Polish lands in the west. He was a pagan, but that would change toward the end of the 980s. Vladimir adopted Orthodox Christianity as the Kievan Rus religion in 988, having rejected Islam and Judaism as possible faiths of the state. It was ultimately the position of Constantinople as the era's central metropolis and the focal point of Byzantium that impressed Vladimir to follow the religion.[14] The Kievan Rus had fought several military campaigns against Byzantium and Constantinople, but Constantinople was ultimately the powerhouse of Europe at the time, making it the center of civilization as far as the Rus were concerned. Therefore, leaders such as Vladimir also sought Byzantine acceptance. According to some historians of Ukraine, this would open the possibility of marriage between Europe's royal families, as all of them were linked to the Church, and the newcomers, the Kievan Rus. Vladimir's decision to convert to Christianity was, therefore, primarily a strategic one. In fact, Vladimir's grandmother, Olga, had converted in Constantinople in the 950s and returned to her homeland, attempting to convert both her family and her people. Her son, Sviatoslav, was firmly committed to his pagan beliefs, and there was substantial resistance to Olga's efforts. Vladimir did, however, convert to Christianity in an attempt to pacify and be accepted by Byzantium. The emperor of Byzantium, Basel II, wanted military support from Vladimir, who in turn requested to marry the emperor's sister, Anna. For this, Vladimir needed to convert to Christianity, which he duly did by being baptized in Crimea in 988.

---

[14] Marr 2012

The Baptism of Saint Prince Vladimir by Viktor Vasnetsov (1890)

Vladimir's choice would have enormous long-term implications for the development of the region. The Kievan Rus would become a stronghold for Byzantium Christianity and subsequently the Orthodox branch of the faith, and centuries later, Russia would view itself as a defender of Orthodox Christians throughout Europe. Bonds were built between the Rus and other believers in eastern and southeastern Europe, including in Greece, Bulgaria, Romania, and Serbia. This would also have significant consequences when Russia took its place as a continental empire in the 19th century.

Greek culture reached Kiev around 1000, and it impacted the region and endured long after the Kievan Rus had faded into history. The familiar domes of the Orthodox churches, other religious practices, as well as the Cyrillic alphabet would all become features of Ukraine and Russia.

In the 11th century, the Rus were led by Yaroslav the Wise from 1019-1054. Yaroslav built churches in the country and encouraged Kiev's development into an imperial capital. By the end of his reign, the Kievan Rus' territory stretched from the Black Sea to the Baltic Sea and as far west as the Carpathian Mountains.

This period is sometimes considered the "golden age" of the Kievan Rus, but the kingdom also began to disintegrate around the middle of the 11th century. This was due to a number of factors, including factionalism within the Kievan Rus. The decline of Constantinople was also key to these developments, as the Rus' economy was dependent on the Byzantine capital's prosperity.

Still, it took a century of declining fortunes to weaken the Kievan Rus enough that it was truly vulnerable to attack from outsiders. Kiev was sacked in 1169 by another Rus faction and was sucked into the Crusades when

Constantinople was attacked in 1204, further devastating the Rus' trade routes. Novgorod also stood apart from the Rus, declaring the Novgorod Republic in 1136. While Novgorod continued to prosper relative to its neighbors, Kiev split into 12 different component regions, which obviously strained everyone and everything involved.

In 1147, Moscow was founded as a Rus settlement that was historically a part of Russia rather than Ukraine. Though this likely seemed relatively unimportant at the time, it represented the expansion of the Rus project and its blurring into separate territories. The Kievan Rus were finally finished off by the Mongol invasions in the 1230s and 1240s.[15]

The Novgorod Republic existed as an autonomous entity until the end of the 15th century, and it was essentially an offshoot of the medieval Kievan Rus. Stretching from the Gulf of Finland to the Ural Mountains across today's northern Russia, the Novgorod Republic was another example of how the Kievan Rus split in the middle ages, from the more or less unified and expanding version to the end of Yaroslav the Wise's reign, at which point it descended into factionalism and splits in the centuries following. Previously, Novgorod had grand princes appointed by Kiev, but in the mid-12th century, it rejected one of them and his alternatives. As a result, Novgorod

---

[15] Hoffman 2008

moved away from the already weakening Kievan Rus kingdom.

Due to its position, the trials and tribulations of Byzantium and Constantinople had less of an impact on Novgorod. Located on the Dnieper River in a strategic position in the north of Rus territory, Novgorod achieved de facto independence when it joined the Hanseatic League, which was based around the Scandinavian, Baltic, and northern German ports. Novgorod diverged further from the Rus during this period due to the Mongol invasions - whereas the Kievan Rus on the land of today's Ukraine were fundamentally changed by the Mongol invasions, Novgorod essentially made a deal with the Mongol khans to pay tribute and become a distant satellite of that kingdom, thus avoiding the violence of an invasion from the Golden Horde.

However, Novgorod, with its key trading position and relative wealth, was eyed by the kingdoms of Poland and Lithuania, as well as the Grand Duchy of Moscow. Thus, Novgorod ultimately became a battleground during the late 13th century, setting the scene for the Battle on the Ice.

The Livonian Brothers Push East

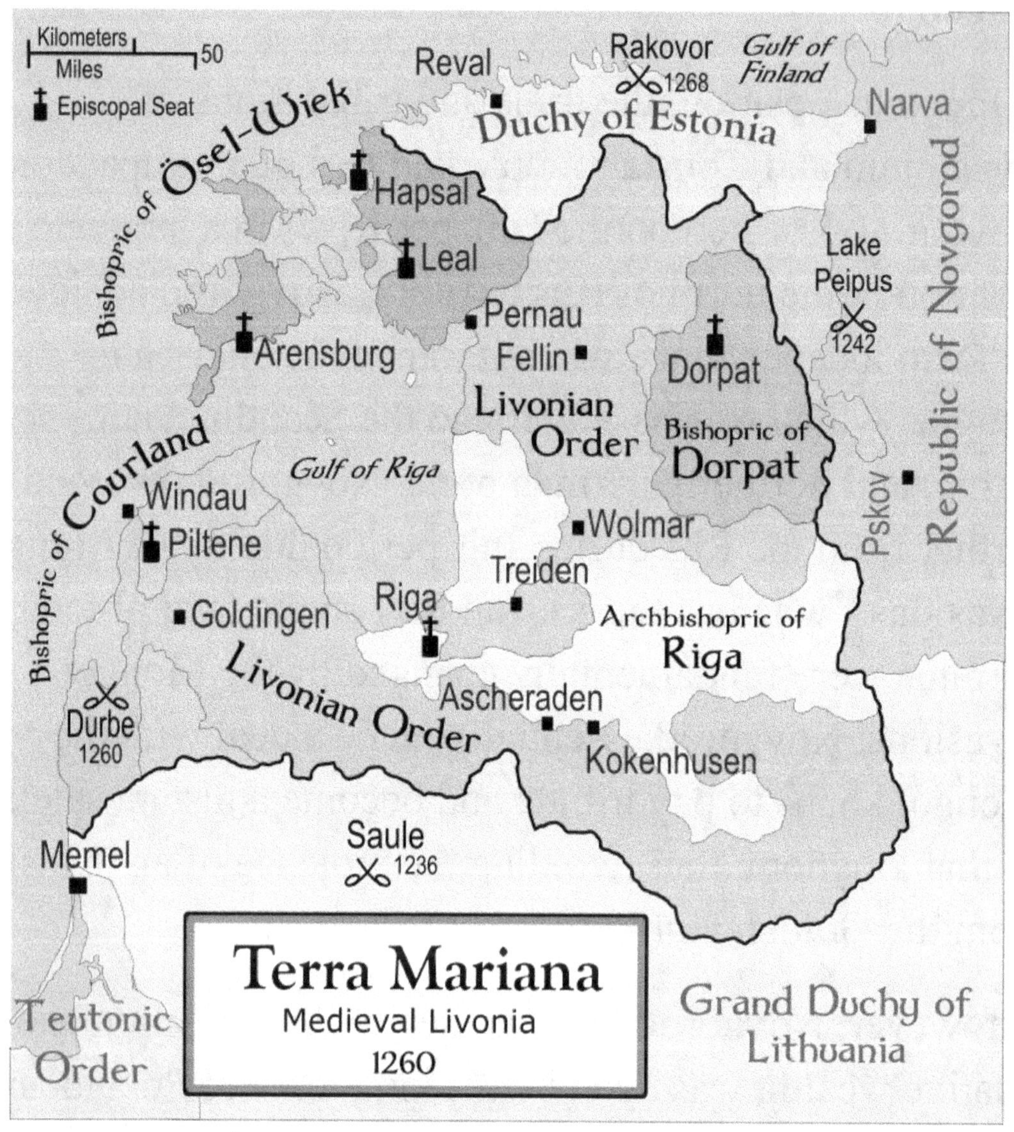

A map of the region in 1260

The Livonian Brothers of the Sword did not participate in any fighting near Jerusalem, but the organization was founded shortly after the papacy called for the First Crusade. While the Crusades are now almost completely associated with the conflicts fought against Muslims to the east, they encompassed other areas as a series of religious wars sanctioned by the Catholic Church against enemies deemed heretical due to their devotion to different gods or failure to uphold the tenets and theology of the Latin institution. A crusade could be called to stamp out Paganism, for example, as with the Livonian Brothers of the Sword in Eastern Europe. The primary targets of the Crusades were Jerusalem in the Middle East and the Eastern Mediterranean, which was threatened by the Islamic Caliphates and the growing Ottoman Empire. It should also be noted that while current historians refer to these holy wars as the Crusades, this term was not popularized until 1760. Contemporary medieval people referred to the actions of the Catholic Church as the religious or holy wars.

The First Crusade established numerous precedents for future holy wars. In particular, pilgrims and crusaders would come from all classes to take public vows and receive plenary indulgences from the Church. Many participants hoped there would be a mass ascension of the faithful to heaven from Jerusalem, and this morphed into the Catholic Church's granting indulgences guaranteeing God's forgiveness for an individual's sins, which became a major draw for nobles and soldiers who worried about the consequences of their plundering and murdering during warfare. Other people joined the Crusades to obtain glory, raise their social status, gain political power, and satisfy obligations to feudal lords, and many of these elements would also ring true for those in the Livonian Brothers of the Sword.

Despite the initial success, the Crusades would ultimately fail, but while the last Catholic outposts in the Middle East fell by the end of the 13th century, outposts continued to exist in Northern and Western Europe, where the enemies were not Muslims and Turks but peoples viewed as pagan and heretical to the Catholic Church. The Wendish Crusade resulted in the groups living in the Northeast Baltic felling under Catholic control, strengthening Central Europe, and in the early 13th century, the Teutonic Order would develop a new Crusader state in Prussia, creating a holy order that defended and controlled much of the Baltic region. The French monarchy also extended its empire through the Albigensian Crusade, which brought French territory straight to the Mediterranean Sea. By 1492, the Christian kingdoms of the Iberian Peninsula managed to throw out the Moors, who had controlled part of the land for over 700 years. That happened to be the same year Columbus sailed east and ended up in the Americas, and from there, interests in conquest moved away from the Mediterranean and across the Atlantic Ocean to the New World.

A map of the Baltic circa 1200

Meanwhile, the Livonian Brothers of the Sword plied Christianity on the eastern shores of the Baltic Sea, primarily in Livonia but also in many other small counties and kingdoms making up the region. Today, the Baltic Sea is enclosed by modern Denmark, Estonia, Finland, Latvia, Lithuania, Sweden, northeast Germany, Poland, Russia, and the North and Central European Plain, and the Livonian Brothers of the Sword's main enemies were native Baltic peoples populating the region and forming small counties of ethnically and culturally similar groups. Ironically, the first foe was the Livonians themselves, who lived close to the north coast of the Baltic Sea and stood in the way of profitable German trade routes. Other enemies living further to the south included the Estonians, Latgalians, Semigallians, Selonians, Curonians, Lithuanians, Skalvians, and Prussians. Over time, as the order grew more powerful, the Livonian Brothers of the Sword would count many native individuals among their allies, especially as regional tensions compelled various indigenous groups to side with the invading Germans in hopes of settling scores and gaining long-desired territory.

The presence of profitable trade routes was the primary reason behind the Catholic Church's desire for control over Eastern Europe. This gave the creation of the Livonian Brothers of the Sword a financial aspect, as many of the knights sought wealth and glory rather than the actual spread of Christianity. Centuries later, Enlightenment thinkers who harbored a healthy skepticism of the Church would note such motivations, and after Voltaire ruefully described the Holy Roman Empire as "neither holy nor Roman nor an empire," the adage has clung to the empire ever since.[16]

However, by the time Voltaire made that observation, the Holy Roman Empire had planted roots in Central

---

[16] Voltaire 1756

Europe nearly 1,000 years earlier, and during the Livonian Brothers of the Sword's existence, the Holy Roman Empire was holy and an empire, albeit no longer Roman in culture or economy. In fact, the Holy Roman Empire was a multiethnic network of territories and provinces throughout Western and Central Europe established in the Early Middle Ages, and it would eventually spread to Eastern Europe and continue to be an influential power until its dissolution in 1806 at the hands of Napoleon.

The largest territory controlled by the empire was the Kingdom of Germany, from which many of the Livonian Brothers of the Sword hailed. Other significant territories included the Kingdom of Bohemia, the Kingdom of Burgundy, and the Kingdom of Italy, which included much of the land near Rome. As such, the empire wielded influence throughout Europe and controlled numerous trade routes, including ones that went through Eastern Europe's pagan lands.

The Vatican crowned the emperor of the Holy Roman Empire and in theory wielded almost absolute power throughout the territories, although he relied upon the local princes to keep the peace. Thus, even as multiple rulers tried to consolidate power on the throne, the empire functioned like a massive bureaucracy rooted in feudalism, giving the knights who joined the Livonian Brothers of the Sword opportunities to carve out spheres of power and influence for themselves.

The Livonian Brothers of the Sword could be considered a Teutonic religious knighthood, and it was established by the third bishop of Riga in 1202. Pope Innocent III sanctioned the establishment of the new order again in 1204, giving the Livonian Brothers more legitimacy. At this time, the majority of the order's membership was comprised of German warrior monks who had gathered to battle nearby Finnic and Baltic pagans inhabiting Latvia, Lithuania, and Estonia. They were thus an Eastern European order, although many of the knights hailed from Central Europe and moved east in an attempt to spread Christianity and the burgeoning power of the Church.

An illustration of a Teutonic Knight on the left and a Swordbrother on the right

The Livonian Crusade led by the order actually began in 1198, four years before the organization was granted legitimacy, and this crusade distinguished itself from other contemporary crusades because "the expeditions which went to Livonia were not accompanied by a papal legate," a standard feature in other holy wars declared by the Catholic Church.17 It also started with a war against the Livonians and Latgalians rather than an initial conflict

---

17 Brundage 1972:4

between Christians and "heretics." Christianity had arrived in Latvia around the 7th century when a group of Swedish settlers built the town of Grobiņa, and its presence was reinforced by the Danes in the 11th century when settlers moved to the area. Christianity, however, was limited to foreign settlements, so many natives continued to practice their original religions.

This would be the situation into which Germans stumbled in the second half of the 12th century when they began trading along one of the most ancient Greek routes, stretching across Varangian territory. Only a small fraction of the indigenous population was baptized, and even fewer adhered to the tenets of the Church.

In 1184, a man named Saint Meinhard of Segeberg made it his mission to convert native Livonians to Christianity. He arrived in the town of Ikšķile and received permission for his work from the Bishop of Uxkull in 1186, and this small settlement was the central driving force of all missionary activities in Livonia in the late 12th century, making it the perfect starting place for Meinhard.

Conversations came easily at first. Native Livonians had lost to the nearby East Slavic Principality of Polotsk and were forced to pay tribute. They were also under attack from the Semigallians to the south and needed allies fast. Thus, when Low Germans like Meinhard, called Saxons, arrived, they seemed like the best choice. The Saxons exerted some influence and clearly had power since they were able to maintain a settlement despite its being in unfriendly territory.

Around 1189, a Livonian leader named Caupo of Turaido would be the first prominent individual to convert, undergoing a full baptism, but few conversions followed. While the local Livonians seemed interested in being baptized, they did not want to adhere to the rules Christianity placed on its followers. Nonetheless, the Livonians helped the missionaries maintain their settlement in exchange for trade and resources for a few years.

The situation grew rapidly dire in 1193, when Pope Celestine III called for a crusade against all pagans in Northern Europe, including native Livonians. Since peaceful conversion had not produce the desired results, Meinhard grew impatient and decided to convert the locals by force.

Initially, Meinhard's attempts to drum up military support failed miserably, and his plot went nowhere. Although he managed to attract a few soldiers and knights among the Saxons, many people refused to come. Instead, knights were far more interested in the defense of Jerusalem, which promised riches and the chance to join a developed institution of knighthood like the Templars or Hospitallers.

Meinhard died a failure in 1196, resulting in the arrival of a replacement in the guise of Bishop Berthold of Hanover, a Cistercian Abbot from Loccum. Berthold brought with him a massive contingent of crusaders intent on beating the pagans back, but he would not last long. He arrived in 1198 and was almost immediately killed in battle after deciding to ride ahead of his troops. The bishop was surrounded and executed by Livonians, after which the rest of the crusaders lost the upper hand and were slaughtered.

Back in Rome, Pope Innocent III grew frustrated. With two men having been killed at the hands of the Livonians, he ramped up his efforts for another crusade, issuing a formal papal bull declaring its beginning against the heretical Livonians. In exchange, he promised soldiers and knights their sins would be forgiven for eliminating the heretics. He also assigned a new leader for the area in the form of Bishop Albrecht von Buxthoeven. Buxthoeven was consecrated as bishop in 1199 and arrived in Livonia at the head of a new contingent of troops larger than the last, establishing Riga as the head of his bishopric in 1201. The following year, he formed the Livonian Brothers, officially beginning the organization in 1202, although its roots could be traced back two decades.

The Livonian Brothers experienced initial, rapid success, sparking rebellions among the Livonians. In response, the Germans tightened their grip on the region, smothering local trade. One of the Christened chiefs, Caupo, led the Livonians against the crusaders in repeated battles over the next three years, and while few records remain about the size of the opposing forces or territory gained or lost, the indigenous Livonians generally struggled against the crusaders. Caupo remained in charge until the Livonians were soundly defeated at Turaida in 1206, when the Christians hailed themselves as victors and the Livonians were made official converts.

In a surprise twist, Caupo accepted his defeat and became an ally of the crusaders until he died in 1217 during the Battle of St. Matthew's Day, which saw the Livonian Brothers and their local allies uniting to combat the counties of Estonia. In that battle, the crusaders sought to stem the tide of German regional control against approximately 6,000 soldiers. The Estonians lost, resulting in their mass baptism and the death of Chieftain Lembitu, one of their best leaders, who had tried to unite the Estonians under a single banner. His death further divided the region, which was great news for the Livonian Brothers, as they quickly took advantage of the splintered area to push German and Christian influence forward.

There was a decade between the Livonian conversion

and the Battle of St. Matthew's Day, and the Swordbrothers used it to consolidate control over the region. By 1208, the Livonian Brothers captured notable Daugava trading posts and renamed them, resulting in the appearance of Holme, Kokenhusen, and Selburg in monastery records. Energetic campaigning also established new local alliances between the Latgalians, an ancient Baltic tribe in Eastern Latvia organized in a series of counties, and the crusaders. After they had allied with the Livonian Brothers, the knights constructed Cesis Castle and Koknese Castle, designed to replace the wooden Latgalian ones. Koknese was to be at the crux of the Daugavlda and Perse Rivers.

The ruins of Koknese Castle

The ruins of Cesis Castle

The Swordbrothers did not form alliances with all Latgalians. Several counties refused to surrender or make a deal, prompting the crusaders to target the nearby Principality of Jersika in 1209, and this situation led to the order's capture of the wife of Visvaldis, the ruler. Visvaldis loved his wife, but he also feared the order's power, so he submitted his kingdom to Bishop Buxthoeven, who merged the kingdom with the Archbishopric of Riga and granted part of it back to Visvaldis as a fief in exchange for loyalty to the Christians.

The other Latgalians faced more issues besides the

Livonian Brothers. The Principality of Talava suffered considerably in wars against the Russians and Estonians. With little hope of remaining independent and wary of losing to their old enemies, Talava's nobles submitted to the crusaders, making it a vassal state of the Archbishopric of Riga around 1214. Talava was eventually divided between the Swordbrothersn and the Archbishopric, giving the Livonian Brothers a greater advantage in the region and putting them at odds with the Estonians, who still wanted the territory.

In the 13th century, the Estonians, one of the oldest Baltic tribes with centuries of infrastructure deeply entrenched in the region, were a major power in Eastern Europe, but by 1208, the crusaders believed they were powerful enough to begin significant operations against the Estonians, utilizing bases established in what was formerly Latgalian territory. At the time, the Estonians possessed eight major counties and seven smaller ones, led by regional elders, but these counties often did not cooperate and remained divided by local differences. They were, however, fierce in their defense against the Livonian Brothers when the crusaders mounted attacks into Sakala and Ugaunia in Southern Estonia. The raids were initially unsuccessful, and the Estonians brutally sacked Riga whenever possible.

As with the battles against the Latgalians and native Livonians, few detailed records remain about the conflict between the Swordbrothers and the Estonians, even though the war raged between 1208 and 1227. While the Livonian Brothers relied upon their vassal states for allies and some of the baptized local leaders, they had to contend with unfaithful allies, most notably the Livonians, Latgalians, and Russians forming the Republic of Novgorod, switching sides between the brotherhood and the Estonians with increasing frequency.

The Livonian Brothers concentrated on attacking Estonian hill forts that formed the centers of the Estonian counties (some historians and anthropologists have compared them to castles). The crusaders besieged the hill forts at every opportunity, resulting in an elaborate game in which the forts were captured, lost, and recaptured again and again until both sides grew weary of war. Eventually, the Swordbrothers entered a three-year truce with the Estonians, lasting from 1213-1215. During this time, the Germans, who formed the majority of the Livonian Brothers, consolidated their political position and stockpiled resources for the inevitable upcoming conflict. The Estonians, however, could not convince the counties to form a consolidated state, no matter how temporary the arrangement.

When the truce ended in 1215, the Swordbrothers had the advantage, and while the crusaders hoped to spread Christianity and eliminate heretics, the knights were more interested in preserving Saxon power in the region and keeping profitable trade routes open because they benefitted from the trade. In addition to bolstering their coffers and those of the Church, their successes acquired more territory in which Christians could settle. Estonia possessed its own allure, with land that could be used to develop new trade routes, so the Swordbrothers began the war against the Estonians, led by Lembitu of Lehola, anew. Lembitu, the elder and leader of Sackalia, the center of Estonian resistance, kept the Estonians strong for six years until the fateful Battle of St. Matthew's Day on September 21, 1217, in which he perished.

A year later, the Livonian Brothers faced new competition from other Christian kingdoms who wanted a piece of Eastern Europe. Denmark and Sweden arrived, eager to expand the eastern coast of the Baltic Sea, and when their forces showed up in 1218, Buxthoeven asked for assistance from King Valdemar II of Denmark. Instead, Valdemar made a deal with the Livonian Brothers, pitting the Church against the rising religious knighthood, which meant the order would need to share its spoils from the war against the Estonians if any were won.

Valdemar II earned some fast victories, including at the Battle of Lindanise in Revelia around the year 1219. Many historians speculate the battle helped to create the

design of the current Flag of Denmark. He also founded
Castrum Danorum, an influential fortress that survived
two sieges by the Estonians in 1220 and 1223.

A modern picture of Castrum Danorum

Meanwhile, King John I of Sweden attempted to
establish a presence in the area by attacking the county of
Wiek, but his troops were assaulted and defeated by local
Oeselians in the Battle of Lihula around 1220. With
Sweden gone, the Swordbrothers and the Danes leaped
upon the rest of northern Estonia, claiming Harrien,
Revelia, and Virumaa over the next three years.

The war would worsen and grow more brutal as the
conflict for Estonia came to a head between 1223 and
1224. The Livonian Brothers, along with their allies, lost
all Christian strongholds in the region except for one, and
all of the defenders were slaughtered. The Estonian

victory would not last, however; in 1224, the crusaders doubled their efforts and took back all of the larger fortresses except Tharbata, which was manned by 200 Russian mercenaries and an angry and determined garrison of Estonian natives who refused to fall to the crusaders' siege. The leader of the Russian mercenaries was an enterprising man named Vyachko, and he had been told he could have the fortress and its nearby land "if he could conquer them for himself."[18] He never got the chance to keep it, as the crusaders returned in late summer to capture the fortress and kill the surviving defenders, including Vyachko.

"Christianizing" Russia

After the taking of Tharbata, Holy Roman Emperor Frederick II announced that Livonia, Prussia, Sambia, and some of the neighboring provinces around the Baltic Sea would be considered *reichsfrei*. Thus, instead of being under the control of local rulers, the officials governing these lands would be subordinates of the Holy Roman Empire and the Catholic Church. Shortly afterward, Pope Honorius III appointed Bishop William of Modena as the papal legate for the region, sending a new priest to be intermediary between the *reichsfrei* and the Church.

---

[18] Arbusow 1982: 246

**Wolfgang Rieger's picture of a contemporary statue
of Emperor Frederick II**

Little changed for the Livonian Brothers despite the
switch in management. The knights of the order were still
called upon to defend trade routes and take new territory,
and many of the soldiers were deeply embedded in the
tricky business of keeping Estonian locals subordinate
while politicians and popes hundreds of miles away
played power politics. To simplify matters, the Livonian
Brothers established a new headquarters at Fellin in
Sackalia and founded several more defensible strongholds

like Wenden, Segewold, and Ascheraden. Knights and clerics could move between the fortresses as needed to maintain the borders of the Christian territories, though frequent raids by displaced Estonians and other peoples were common. Pilgrimages to Eastern Europe picked up around 1224 and 1225, meaning Christians from Western Europe came to see relics and visit churches.

By the time the Livonian Brothers had merged with the Teutonic Knights, the Teutonic Knights had crushed, conquered, and now held reign over 5 of the 7 principal Prussian regions, such as Bartia, Warmia, Pomesania, Poegesania, and Natangia, spawning what collectively came to be called the "Monastic State of the Teutonic Order." Pope Gregory IX's *Golden Bull of Rieti* confirmed the order's possession over the newly risen crusader state, and allowed it to do as it wished so long as it paid its respects to the pope. About 7 years into the Prussian conquest, membership experienced another jump when the order brought into the fold the Livonian Brothers of the Sword (or the Livonian Sword Brethren), a military-religious brotherhood founded by the Bishop of Riga, as well as the Polish-born Order of Dobrzyn, making the organizations a part of its entity.

To combat Prussia's population problem, which was in danger of dying out due to revolts, invasions, and the evils of the plague, the knights decided to furnish the place with new colonists, just as they had in Burzenland. As they continued to address the pagan issue, shiploads of Catholic colonists from Belgium, Poland, Germany, the Netherlands, and other lands of the Holy Roman Empire spilled onto the Prussian shore. The knights wasted no time in reaching out to the colonists for their help in establishing castles and forts to secure their new plots of conquered land.

The order's controversial conversion tactics were as savage as they were black and white. A Prussian captive's baptism was their only hope of release and maintaining some sort of normalcy in their life under the stifling Teutonic reign. Those who so much as protested were either put down or forever banished from their homelands. This was not to say the Prussians accepted their new fates; on the contrary, the boldest of the bunch who refused to lose their culture squared off against the knights, with quite a few succeeding in "roasting captured brethren alive in their armor, like chestnuts, before the shrine of a local god."

Uprisings became unavoidable in this feral and treacherous climate, and during its Prussian reign, a total of 5 full-fledged insurgencies threatened to topple everything the knights had built thus far. The second revolt, now remembered as the infamous "Great Prussian Uprising" of 1260, was the largest and most severe of its kind, claiming the most Teutonic casualties. At least 150 knights allegedly perished in a single session, a sobering figure that only paled in comparison to the unknown number of lives lost to the Teutonic sword in the 13th century. By the time the last uprising in 1295 had wound down, the German language had become the official language in what was now a mainly Christian Prussia.

Mariusz Kędzierski's picture of the ruins of the Teutonic castle in Rehden, one of five castles not captured by the Prussians

The fast-paced growth of the monastic state might have been applauded by the papacy and most European Christians, but many did not hesitate to shine a light on the knights' unorthodox military techniques and callous treatment of the pagan Prussians. These naysayers accused the knights of taking the Lord's word out of context to justify all the bloodshed and heartache they caused. One of the most vocal critics of the time was the celebrated English philosopher, Roger Bacon, who chose to use his platform to raise awareness of the order's misdeeds in 1266. Said Bacon, "[T]he brothers of the Teutonic Order much disturb the conversion of infidels because of the wars which they are always starting, and because of the fact that they wish to dominate them absolutely...The pagan race has many times been ready to receive the faith in peace after preaching, but those of the Teutonic order do not wish to allow this, because they wish to subjugate them and reduce them to slavery." Women and children were not spared either, since the order perceived them as little more than human, and as such, "not worthy of life."

By the mid-13th century, as the Livonian Brothers were struggling, the superiors of the Teutonic Order had already been briefed about the weakened state of Russia, and they, too, wanted in on what they saw as a territorial free-for-all. Their plans were met with the enthusiastic support of Pope Gregory IX, who encouraged the knights to set forth and "Christianize" Russia. In 1240, a Teutonic-sponsored army of German, Danish, and

Estonian knights, ex-Livonian Sword Brethren, and Russian renegades burst into the city of Pskov and held it hostage. There, they captured the Bjorg Castle and effortlessly vanquished its inhabitants. Thrilled with the cakewalk of a victory, they left behind only 50 attendants and 2 knights to hold down the new fort.

A Renaissance depiction of Pope Gregory IX

There is some confusion as to whether the papal legate in Livonia, William of Modena (c. 1184–1251) did actually proclaim a crusade against Orthodox Novgorod in the pope's name. It seems that Gregory's response to the

Novgorodian threat may not have been a direct proclamation of a crusade against the republic but against the Finns, where the Christian missions established by the Swedes were under attack from Novgorod.[19] Whatever the truth of the matter, the interested parties in the Baltic – Sweden, the Teutonic-Livonian Order, and the Hanseatic League – seem to have been under the impression that William had sanctioned military action against the Rus and responded accordingly.[20]

The Opposing Forces

Alexander Nevsky was the second son of the Grand Prince of the Rus Yaroslav II Vsevolodovich (r. 1238–1246) and Fedosia Igorevna. His father was ruler of all Russia in name only, which in effect was a collection of autonomous principalities. As ruler of the most powerful, Vladimir-Suzdal, Yaroslav could claim pre-eminence, and when the Golden Horde invaded in 1236 Batu Khan was pleased to confirm him in return for a pledge to serve the Horde and collect its tribute from the other princes. Before reigning as Grand Prince he governed Novgorod and then Kiev, leaving Alexander, only 15, as prince in Novgorod.

It has already been noted that Novgorod the Great was not technically a monarchy. As the great empire of the

[19] Kari, Risto (2000). *Suomalaisten keskiaika*. WS Bookwell Oy. Porvoo, p.107.
[20] Nicolle, p.47.

Rus weakened and power shifted from the ancient capital of Kiev to the regional princes, the Novgorodians elected to dismiss their own, Vsevold of Pskov (r. 1117–1132). Thereafter the city and its vast dominions was ruled by the *Veche,* which elected a *posadnik* (executive officer) from the ranks of the boyars, who shared authority with the archbishop, also elected by the *Veche.* The office of *Knez* was not abolished, but his functions were limited to commanding the republic's armies and executing the laws. His office was not hereditary, and he could be – and frequently was – expelled, if it appeared as though he was growing too powerful. This was why Prince Alexander was dismissed after his victory at the Battle of the Neva. Despite his extreme youth, Alexander rapidly proved a military leader of uncommon ability as well as an astute politician.

The Russian military at this time was based on the *druzhina* system. A *druzhina* (literally "fellowship") was a prince's retinue, and both fought with him and assisted him in the administration of his territory. Members could be high-born *boyars* or lesser freemen. The boyars were intimate members of the prince's household while the junior members were armed retainers. They were bound not by land as in the feudal West but by an oath of personal loyalty to the prince, which could in fact be withdrawn if his fortunes waned or if he was defeated in battle.

The boyar core of the *druzhina* was composed of heavy cavalry armoured like their Scandinavian forebears in conical helmets, padded armour and chainmail. They were armed with long spears, curved swords, bows and maces and their steeds were often armoured. In addition there were city militias raised by the city *veche*, but these were drawn from the small middle class of merchants, craftsmen and artisans and were thus limited in their effectiveness. They were infantry and comprised the bulk of an army's infantry. They usually wore no armour and used axes and hunting spears, but not swords. These militias were raised in emergencies but for organized campaigns a prince and his *druzhina* were called upon. The peasantry or *smerdi* could also be called upon, though peasant soldiers were even less effective than the militia.

An important element of the Russian military was not Russian at all. Before the Mongol invasion, the southern steppes were inhabited by several semi-nomadic peoples of the Turkic language group and included the Kipchaks, Cumans, Berendei, Torkil and Pechenegs. When the Mongols invaded, most of these tribes were absorbed into the Golden Horde. Others entered into the service of the Russian princes and were referred to as *Chernye Klobuki*, the "Black Hats." Sometimes the Mongols themselves would assist their Russian vassals, for it was in their interest to support the princes who provided regular tribute. Yet even without considering a Turkic or Mongol element, Alexander's army would not have been ethnically homogenous. Many *druzhina* would have been composed of Finns, Karelians, Balts, Ingrians and other Finno-Ugrians. These were mostly hunter-gatherers who inhabited the forests and swamps of Novgorod's hinterland and were skilled in ambush and skirmishing.

Orthodoxy has often been portrayed as a peace-loving religion that found the crusading ideal of Western Christianity abhorrent[21] and this may have been true of the Byzantines but less so of the Rus, whose Slavic and Varangian (Scandinavian) forebears both produced strong military cultures. In particular, Russian Orthodoxy cherished the concept of the warrior-saint who defended the true faith and its adherents against its enemies. Many Orthodox saints were portrayed as warriors and Alexander Nevsky himself was canonized. And so, the army of Rus faced the Germanic force with a motivation every bit as powerful as that of Western crusaders.

The forces of the crusaders were modeled largely on those of North Germany and Denmark. Most belong to the Teutonic and Livonian Orders, and it will be remembered that the much-reduced Brothers of the Sword were absorbed into the Teutonic Order. Even so, they formed a

---

[21] David Nicolle (1997), *Lake Peipus 1242: Battle of the Ice*, Osprey Publishing p.37.

tiny elite drawn from the minor German aristocracy. They were not expected to display the usual monastic qualities of piety and meekness but were received into the Order for their more martial characteristics. The crusade in the north required warriors and the Order could not afford to be too selective. Even so, they were required to observe poverty, chastity and obedience, at least in theory. Young men often joined the crusading orders for noble ideals but there were other attractions as well. Many of the lesser German nobility were poor and could not afford to support all their sons. A career in the Church or a military order was an assurance of regular meals and status in medieval society. The prospect of adventure and glory must have been attractive to many youths as well.

The supreme authority in the Teutonic state (*Ordenstaat*), beneath the pope, was the General Chapter, consisting of 12 senior knights, one of whom was elected Grandmaster (*Hochmeister*). The grandmaster was not a cleric – the Order consisted of laymen in character except for chaplains – and not a monarch: his decisions were limited and frequently challenged. The General Chapter oversaw the three chapters governing Prussia, Livonia and the other territories and houses (mostly in Germany); each was presided over by a Master. The general headquarters of the Ordenstaat was at the fortress of Marienburg (Malbork). The basic unit of administration was the commandery, where the commander (*komtur*) behaved much like a feudal lord, protecting the local population, receiving taxes and administering justice. The knights under his command lived in community, eating and praying in the Divine Office (official prayer of the Church) together.

There were four grades of Teutonic Knights. The first were the aristocratic knight-brothers and they alone held administrative posts. Then there were the priest-brothers, much less numerous, who served as military chaplains but were prohibited by their holy orders to shed blood. The Sariant or serving brothers were the most numerous and were recruited from the local population. They constituted the bulk of Teutonic armies and were distinguished from the knight-brothers and priest-brothers by their grey, rather than white, tunics. The fourth grade in the Teutonic Order made up the half-brothers and consisted of servants, agriculturalists and tradesmen.

The Teutonic Knights did not observe standard monastic ordinances owing to the martial nature of their existence. Fasting and abstinence from meat was observed only on the Mondays, Wednesdays, Fridays and Saturdays of Lent, and in Advent (December). Individual attempts to emulate the austerities of other orders were despised as vainglorious and deleterious, as every knight had to be fit for battle at any moment.

Artillery such as ballistae and trebuchets did not form a large part of the knights' armory, though they were perfectly capable of besieging enemy fortresses. They were better skilled in defensive siege warfare[22] – they built fortresses in tribal territories and defended them until their attackers were weakened and vulnerable. Artillery would not be a factor in the Battle on the Ice.

Mention should also be made of the secular knights, minor German lords who settled in Prussia and Livonia but without making vows to the Order. These held fiefs from the Order and were obliged to come to its aid in time of war. These individuals were often the younger scions of the German nobility who could not hope to share in the riches and honor of their older brothers.

The strengths and skills of the Teutonic military were shaped by their experience of Baltic warfare. The terrain was dominated by thick forests and marshes which favored the indigenous light cavalry and infantry who could strike suddenly and swiftly and then disappear into the woods. The knights wearing heavy armor were frequently at a disadvantage and they rapidly learned to use lighter native conscripts or mercenaries to flank their enemies in open combat while the knights themselves held the center.[23] This tactic was effective in open battle

---

[22] David Nicolle (2007) *Teutonic Knight 1190–1561*, Osprey Publishing Great Britain, p.48.
[23] Ibid. p.50.

and close combat but not in forests, marshy ground or on ice, and the knights tended to avoid pitched battles. Conflicts such as the Battle of Lake Peipus were rare. Indeed, ancient and medieval armies in general avoided major clashes. As one strategy manual put it, "To try simply to overpower the enemy in the open, hand to hand and face to face, even though you might appear to win, is an enterprise which is very risky and can result in serious harm. Apart from extreme emergency, it is ridiculous to try to gain victory which is too costly and brings only empty glory."[24]

Risking an army in open combat and surrendering it to fortune was considered foolhardy, even by skilled and experienced generals, and medieval commanders preferred to achieve their goals by less perilous stratagems: "It is good if your enemies are harmed either by deception or raids, or by famine; and continue to harass them more and more, but do not challenge them in open war, because luck plays as a major role as valor in battle."[25]

In this light, the Battle of Lake Peipus was a necessity as far as the knights and their allies were concerned. For the most part, their conquests were achieved by a series of strategic skirmishes, ambushes and sieges.[26]

---

[24] Emperor Maurice, *Strategikon,* c.600 https://www.medievalists.net/2019/08/why-battles-could-be-so-decisive-in-the-middle-ages/.

[25] Emperor Leo VI, *Taktika,* c.900 https://www.medievalists.net/2019/08/why-battles-could-be-so-decisive-in-the-middle-ages/.

All members of the Order bore the distinctive black crusaders' cross on their surcoats. Armor consisted of typical Western chainmail with steel helmets, and weapons included the lance, sword, mace and crossbow, which had superseded the composite bow in most armies, with England being a famous exception.

The Ordenstaat could also call upon their secular vassals for military service. The Order did not generally call upon the local Baltic peoples to fight. In Prussia the knights almost exterminated the population[27] and in Livonia the indigenous inhabitants were still unruly. Still, select converts were called to service, though they would have been poorly trained and equipped. These levies functioned as mounted infantry and scouts. The German-speaking town militias were also of dubious value, though they might be summoned in emergencies.

The Teutonic Knights maintained a strict discipline that gave them an advantage over most other soldiers. The rigor of monastic life was translated to the battlefield: regulations governed every aspect of life in field from sentry duty to the hearing of Mass on campaign. The concept of religious members bearing arms and taking lives naturally raised ethical questions which became the subject of heated debate. Spiritual authorities during the

---

[26] William Urban (1973) "Victims of the Baltic Crusade" and "The Organization and Defense of the Livonian Frontier in the Thirteenth Century," *Speculem* 48, no. 3.

[27] P. Dollinger (1999) *The Herman Hansa*, Routledge p.34.

time of the Roman Empire were divided on whether it was even lawful for Christians to bear arms at all, but medieval Catholic theologians settled on a doctrine that justified defensive war only, and then only under strict conditions.[28] What was clearly an offensive campaign in the Baltic lands was justified in the latter terms by arguing that the crusaders were defending missionary clerics and the few converts that they had made. But as this argument rapidly wore thin, the Church tended to turn a blind eye, albeit with occasional reproaches.[29] A number of contemporaries opined that the crusade against the heathen was to many justified by economic gain more than concern for the salvation of souls.[30] The medieval Church – contrary to a popular misconception – did not approve of forced conversions.[31] One English Franciscan

[28] War had to be declared by a legitimate authority and only to right a wrong when every other avenue of recourse had failed. The sufferance of that wrong however had to be considered a worse evil than that which might be inflicted by war. Civilians could not be harmed and the use of violence had to be proportionate to the end desired, though of course what is considered 'proportionate' was often a matter of debate. *"War,"* (1914) *Catholic Encyclopedia* vol. 15, The Encyclopedia Press, New York.

[29] The Papacy occasionally censured the Teutonic and Livonian Knights. For example in 1230 the ruler of Courland agreed to be baptised and then placed his land under the protection of Pope Gregory IX in order to escape the wrath of the Livonian Order. But the latter attacked him anyway, looting Courland and massacring its inhabitants. Mara Kalnins (2015), *Latvia: A Short History*, Oxford University Press.

[30] Dainius Tomas Delcytus (2014) "The military ethics of the Teutonic Knights," *Encyclopedia of Military Ethics*, https://www.militaryethics.org/The-military-ethics-of-the-Teutonic-Knights/18/.

[31] Nevertheless once converted – however unjustly – forced individuals were bound to at least outwardly observe the practices of Christianity. 'Those who are immersed even though reluctant, do belong to ecclesiastical jurisdiction at least by reason of the sacrament, and might therefore be reasonably compelled to observe the rules of the Christian Faith. It is, to be sure, contrary to the Christian Faith that anyone who is unwilling and wholly opposed to it should be compelled to adopt and observe Christianity. For this reason a valid distinction is made by some between kinds of unwilling ones and kinds of compelled ones. Thus one who is drawn to Christianity by violence, through fear and through torture, and receives the sacrament of Baptism in order to avoid loss, he (like one who comes to Baptism in dissimulation) does receive the impress of Christianity, and may be forced to observe the Christian Faith as one who expressed a conditional willingness though, absolutely speaking, he was unwilling.' Pope Innocent III, Chazan, Robert, ed., Church, State, and Jew in the Middle Ages,

friar observed in 1266, "The brothers of the Teutonic order much disturb the conversion of infidels because of the wars which they are always starting, and because of the fact that they wish to dominate them absolutely. ... The pagan race has many times been ready to receive the faith in peace after preaching, but those of the Teutonic order do not wish to allow this, because they wish to subjugate them and reduce them to slavery."[32]

There was, however, little the Church could do to protect the indigenous peoples and the most it did was occasionally check the excesses of the crusaders. This task was made doubly difficult when the authorities tasked with moderating the Order were themselves crusaders. Such was the case with Albert the Archbishop of Riga and his brother Hermann, Bishop of Dorpat.

The Baltic trade attracted hanseatic merchants to Prussia and Livonia and these often maintained armed retinues or hired mercenaries for their protection. The Catholic Church ruled about half the land in Livonia and the bishops too could call upon their vassals in time of war. The largest ecclesiastical territory was the Archbishopric of Riga which encompassed much of Central Livonia, with the Bishopric of Dorpat extending from Lake Wirzsee (Vortsjav) to Lake Peipus. The Bishopric of

West Orange, NJ: Behrman House, 1980, p.103.

[32] Bridges, John Henry Ed. (1964) The Opus Majus of Roger Bacon Oxford, 1877–1900, repr. Frankfurt, 1964 vol. 3, p.121–2, part 3, ch. 13. (translated by Helen J. Nicholson).

Piltene was in Courland and the Bishop of Osel-Wiek ruled the islands of Saaremaa and western Estonia. The King of Denmark, who directly ruled the Duchy of Estonia, could also call his vassals to arms.

The Battle on the Ice is often portrayed as an epic clash between Russia and the Teutonic Knights, due largely to Eisenstein's *Alexander Nevsky*. In fact, the bulk of the force that challenged Alexander was composed of the vassals and levies of Bishop Hermann of Dorpat, totaling about 300 German knights and around 1,000 indigenous levies. The Duchy of Estonia might have contributed about 200 knights. The total size of the crusader army was probably just short of 2,000, of which the Teutonic (including Livonian) Knights would have made up a fraction. The Order did not even lead the battle, that distinction being claimed by Bishop Hermann himself.

Hermann came from Buxhovden in the Duchy of Saxony where his family exerted considerable influence. His younger brother Albert had been made Bishop of Riga through the intervention of his uncle Hartwig, the Archbishop of Bremen and Hamburg. However, he needed to conquer it first and led a crusade to Livland in 1200. It was Albert who created the Livonian Brothers of the Sword in order to secure his conquests. He invited his brother to assume the new Bishopric of Dorpat as its temporal and spiritual lord in 1220, though he only arrived in 1224.

The concept of the crusade brought up the question of clerics bearing arms. Canon law strictly forbade them to shed blood and any cleric dying in battle might be refused burial rites, though some leeway seems to have been allowed in the case of fighting the enemies of the Church.[33] To the indigenous Livonians and certainly to the Orthodox Rus, the sight of a bishop preaching the love of God and then plunging a sword into his enemy's body seemed puzzling to say the very least.

Alexander Nevsky's force, consisting primarily of his own *druzhina* and that of his brother Andrey, Prince of Suzdal, seems to have been considerably larger than Hermann's, possibly numbering five or six thousand.[34] There were likely a large number of Finnish and Ugrian levies, but there were likely only a few hundred Turkic horse archers.

[33] Frederick H. Russell (1975) *The Just War in the Middle Ages* Cambridge University Press, p.108.
[34] Nicolle, p.41.

The Battle on the Ice

A view of the lake from Estonia in the summer

In 1237 the Mongols initiated their full-scale invasion and devastation of southern Russia, and the crusaders believed it was the ideal time to attack Novgorod, but the Mongol army did not march north into the lands of the republic and would never do so. In 1238, William of Modena toured northern Europe, forging a coalition which included the Teutonic Knights, Denmark, Sweden, Holstein and the prince-bishops of Livonia.

King Eric IX (1216–1250) of Sweden made the first

move in the crusade. He strengthened the Swedish presence in southwestern Finland, expelled the Orthodox missionaries, and helped the (pagan) Finnish tribes fighting Novgorod. Then he launched a naval invasion of Novgorod itself and seized control of the town of Ladoga, near the lake of the same name about 40 kilometers south of modern St Petersburg. It was a vital trading post for Novgorod, situated on the Neva River, connecting the Baltic Sea to Lake Ladoga and Novgorod to the Baltic. The Swedes were led by Bishop Thomas of Finland, a prelate of whom little is known, and Birger, a Swedish Earl (*Jarl*). Their adversary was one Alexander Yaroslavich, Prince (*Knez*) of Novgorod, summoned by its leaders to defend Novgorod. Novgorod was governed by a *Veche* or public assembly made up of the mercantile classes and a council of boyars, with the Archbishop of Novgorod as the republic's titular head. The Veche elected a prince who led the republic's army and executed the laws. He was sent by the Grand Prince of the Rus, who at this time was Yaroslav II. Alexander was his second son.

A painting of the Veche in Novgorod

On July 15, 1240, the allied and Novgorod armies met at the confluence of the Rivers Neva and Izhora, where the latter achieved the victory that earned him the epithet *Nevsky* ("the Great"). The Swedes, surprised at dawn, were driven back to their boats with the loss of only twenty Novgorodians. The 15th century *Chronicle of Novgorod* described the campaign: "Swedes came with a great army,
and Norwegians and Finns and Tavastians with ships in great numbers, Swedes with their prince and bishops, and they stayed on the Neva, at the mouth of the Izhora, willing to take Ladoga, and to put it short, Novgorod and

all of its lands. But still protected the merciful, man-loving God us and sheltered us from the foreign people, and the word came to Novgorod that Swedes were sailing to Ladoga; but prince Alexander did not hesitate at all, but went against them with Novgorodians and people of Ladoga and overcame them with the help of Saint Sophia and through prayers of our lady, the Mother of
God and Virgin Mary, 15 July, in the memory of Kirik and Ulita, on Sunday, (the same day that) the 630 holy fathers held a meeting in Chalcedon; and there was a great gathering of the Swedes; and their leader called Spiridon was killed there; but some claimed that even the bishop was slain; and a great number of them fell; and when they had loaded two ships with the bodies of high-born men, they let them sail to the sea; but the others, that were unnumbered, they cast to a pit, that they buried, and many others were wounded; and that same night they fled, without waiting for the Monday light, with shame. Of Novgorodians there fell: Konstantin Lugotinitch, Yuryata Pinyashchinich, Namest Drochilo, Nesdylov son of Kozhevnik, but including the people of Ladoga 20 men or less, God knows. But Prince Alexander came back home with Novgorodians and people of Ladoga, all well, protected by God and Saint Sophia and all the prayers of the holy men.”[35]

[35] *Chronicle of Novgorod*
https://web.archive.org/web/20070927051426/http://193.184.161.234/DF/detail.php?id=83.

A portrait of Alexander Nevsky

Alexander was given no opportunity to follow up on his victory or to attack the Germanic crusaders then gathering in Livonia and Estonia. The Germanophile boyars clashed with Alexander and forced him to leave the republic. Shortly thereafter the Teutonic and Livonian Orders, along with their hanseatic allies and Livonian bishoprics, invaded, capturing the Russian fortress of Izborsk just south of Lake Peipus. This threatened Pskov, a small Russian principality and trading partner of the Hanseatic

League nominally dependent on Novgorod. In August the crusaders bribed the governor of Pskov into surrendering the city, while from Danish Estonia they advanced east, taking the town of Koporye, where they erected a stone fortress. They then pushed south toward Novgorod and pillaged as far as Tesov. At the same time a small fleet sent by Heinrich the Bishop of Osel (Saaremaa) moved into the Gulf of Finland to blockade Novgorod's trading posts. Heinrich was so confident of a resounding victory that he journeyed to Rome to petition the pope to make him bishop of all the Russian lands yet to be conquered. Indeed there was every reason to believe that Novgorod would fall. The city's leaders had not expected an invasion and they had no prince to defend them. Novgorod's militia was unequal to the task of defeating western knights which were now only fifty kilometers north of Novgorod.

A respite of sorts came when the Mongol Horde, which had still not turned north toward Novgorod, swept Central Europe, invading Hungary and Poland. The northern crusade paused, torn between pressing onto Novgorod or coming to the aid of their fellow Catholics. Pope Gregory IX urged the Teutonic Knights on the matter, but they were divided, and at the Battle of Liegnitz (Legnica) in April 1241 there were no Teutons present.[36] The Mongols

---

[36] William Urban (2003). *The Teutonic Knights: A Military History*. Greenhill Books. London.

were victorious, and it was only the death of the Great Khan Ogedei at Karakorum in December 1241 that halted their advance.

By the spring of 1241, the pro-German faction in Novgorod was silenced and the city begged the 20-year-old prince to return. The Grand Prince was unwilling to return his gifted son to the city that had displayed such ingratitude, so he sent his older son and the Prince of Suzdal, Andrey, instead. But the Novgorodians would have no-one but Alexander and Andrey left after only four months. At length Yaroslav II relented and sent his son north. Alexander had his own price for resuming the princedom: the heads of those who had opposed him in 1240. After hanging many of his enemies, he led his *druzhina* (military entourage) against the foreigners. In the autumn of 1241 he recaptured Koporye with the aid of local tribesmen and with little opposition. Some of the *nemstky* (Germans) were freed, but all those who had joined with the invaders – mostly Estonians – were hanged.

Alexander then marched south toward Pskov in the winter of 1241. The garrison there was still minimal and the prince's advance was wholly unexpected. Until Alexander's return, the crusaders were confident of taking Novgorod and so would not have taken much care in bolstering their fortifications. The prince must have wished to deal the crusaders a crushing blow, for the hitherto rejected Andrey returned with his own Suzdal *druzhina,* producing a force more than sufficient if they had merely wished to regain Pskov. In fact, the fortress was only held by a few Teutonic Knights and a handful of Pskovians and fell with barely a struggle on March 5.

The fall of Pskov was a severe blow to the crusaders, for the Novgorodians could now invade Livonia at will. There was some urgency in meeting the threat, for the spring thaw would turn the hitherto frozen roads to mud. But Alexander was faced with the same necessity and set off along the road to Livonia in March 1242, bypassing the crusader-held fortress of Izborsk. He marched north toward Dorpat (Tartu), seat of Prince-Bishop Hermann von Buxhovden (1163–1248), pillaging as he went. It seems Alexander's intention was not to conquer Livonia and Estonia but merely to leave the knights so weakened that they could not threaten Novgorod.[37] The crusaders succeeded in halting a portion of the advancing host at a bridge at Mooste, some forty-three kilometers south-east of Dorpat. The defeat was not decisive however, and the survivors returned to Alexander and the main force. Aware that Bishop Hermann was rallying his vassals and sending word to the Teutonic Knights, he decided to withdraw across the narrow channel at Mehikoorma,

---

[37] Riley-Smith Jonathan Simon Christopher (1987) *The Crusades: A History*, USA, p.198.

which joined the frozen lakes Pskov and Peipus. Hermann tried unsuccessfully to prevent his retreat and then waited for the rest of his vassals and the Teutonic Knights to arrive. Alexander remained on the Novgorod side of Lake Peipus, only a few kilometers distant.

The climax of the film *Alexander Nevsky* depicts the fleeing German army swallowed up by the freezing waters of Lake Peipus as the ice breaks beneath it. While it was true that the lake was frozen at the time (as it still is in winter), the prospect of fighting on that ice was not as daunting as it might first appear. Alexander's army is believed to have crossed Peipus at its narrowest point at Mehikoorma, measuring less than five kilometers wide and no more than two meters deep. The lake's average depth is seven meters. The ice at Mehikoorma then was likely to be quite thick and the spring thaw generally does not begin until late April.[38] It possibly began later in the 13th century when temperatures began to drop markedly.[39]

Even so, Alexander and his army withdrew not into the lake itself but to the eastern, Novgorodian bank which was a frozen marshland. Rather than picturing a frozen white surface as the "field" of battle, it may be more helpful to imagine a landscape of thin but solid, jagged ice (made so by winds) from which beds of reeds protrude.

---

[38] Sokolov AA *Hydrography of the USSR* L.: Gidrometeoizdat, 1952.
[39] Ladurie, Emmanuel Le Roy (1971). *Times of Feast, Times of Famine: A History of Climate Since the Year 1000*. Barbara Bray. Garden City, NY: Doubleday.

Hermann probably crossed the lake several kilometers north of Mehikoorma in an attempt to outflank the Rus. It would have been deeper there, but even so, scouts with years of local experience would not have advised a crossing if it was dangerous.

Neither the German nor the Russian chroniclers are helpful in locating the battle precisely, but most historians believe it occurred at a place called Raven's Rock, on a peninsula jutting toward Piirissaaar Island.[40] They argue that when the Rus turned to face the crusaders, this would have been the most tactically advantageous place to do so. The westward coastline, lined with jagged ice floes and impenetrable reeds, would have provided natural fortifications, and a retreating enemy would be forced into the lake without any protection. More importantly, a group of islets immediately to the north made it difficult for the attacking army to outflank the Rus.

The battle began at sunrise with the Germans attacking first. Bishop Hermann probably commanded the right flank with his vassal knights, with the Danes or the Teutonic Knights in the center. The indigenous infantry levy brought up the rear.[41] Prince Alexander probably assumed the standard Russian battle position: infantry militia in the center, flanked by cavalry and with

[40] Nicolle, p.71.
[41] Nicolle, p.73.

Alexander and his personal *druzhina* guard in the rear. The Danish knights attempted to attack the Russian right flank through open ice, between Ravens Rock and Piirissaar and were met by the Turkic horse archers who delivered hails of arrows while staying out of reach. The northern crusaders would never have experienced this kind of enemy before and would have not have known how to react except to pursue them.

The rest of the crusader army charged upon the Rus but were hampered by ice floes and reed banks. The local levies fled – if indeed they ever participated in the battle – and it is easy to surmise that they realized that attacking a numerically superior foe in such a naturally-fortified position was the height of folly. With the Danes drawn off by the horse-archers, Hermann's knights and the Teutonic Knights found themselves surrounded. Fighting on the slippery ice proved more exhausting for the crusaders than for the Russians, for the latter had more experience with winter warfare than the German and Danish immigrants.

After enduring heavy casualties, the bishop finally gave the command to break out and retreat in as orderly a manner as possible. They succeeded in escaping but in considerable disarray. They had no choice but to retreat across the open ice. The Teutonic and Livonian Knights in the center probably fled directly west, the way they came, while the Bishop of Dorpat and his knights retreated across Mehikoorma.[42] What remained of the Danes ran west from Piirissaaar Island. Alexander's troops pursued the crusaders across the lake. Hermann and his vassals probably reached the safety of the forest north of Mehikoorma,[43] and the depiction of the bishop drowning in *Alexander Nevsky* is not correct as he died six years after the battle. The Teutonic Knights reached the western shore of Lake Peipus and Alexander probably did not pursue them far into the reed beds.

Predictably, the casualty figures differ according to the side narrating the story. In the 15th century *First Chronicle*, the Russians claimed that 400 Germans and Danes and "countless' Estonians were killed, including 20 elite Teutonic Knights. Six knights were taken prisoner.[44] The *Rhymed Chronicle*, composed in the 14th century to be read in Teutonic monasteries, mentions the death of only the 20 knights, with another six being captured.[45] Setting aside the fact that both accounts were written more than 200 years after the event, both seem exaggerated,[46] though the fact both mention the 20 slain and six captured knights would seem to indicate that those figures are probably correct. What is clear is that the crusaders had suffered a humiliating and costly defeat and that the

---

[42] Nicolle, p.76–77.
[43] Ibid.
[44] *The Chronicle of Novgorod* London. 1914. p.87.
[45] Urban, William (2003). *The Teutonic Knights: A Military History*. Greenhill Books. London.
[46] Nicolle, p.78.

crusade against Novgorod was effectively over.

Alexander did not intend to conquer Livonia but rather defend Novgorod by dealing the *nemstky* a crushing blow, and in that he succeeded. He might have invaded Livonia and might have succeeded in a military sense, but the rulers of Novgorod were wary of a successful prince, which is why Alexander was exiled after Neva, and they would probably have not tolerated the creation of an empire dependent solely upon the prince. The conquest of Livonia would also have attracted hundreds of German knights intent on recovering land lost to the schismatics, backed by a papacy that was relentless toward the perceived enemies of the faith.

Alexander may well have been considering the undesirability of a perpetual war with the West when he returned to Novgorod. On the way, he marched through Pskov and received the submission of its leaders, likely more fearful than grateful, but he did not enter Novgorod with complete confidence. With the spring thaws approaching, Novgorod was safe from a Mongol attack for the time being, but surely, they would invade in the summer, and Alexander knew he could not prevail.

To the west, the Germans were losing their enthusiasm for the crusade against the Rus. Bishop Hermann had time to consider the folly of challenging a numerically superior foe in circumstances where the odds were clearly against the crusaders. Perhaps their earlier victories had persuaded them that Alexander's recapture of Pskov was an atypical aberration. Perhaps Hermann had no inkling that Alexander possessed the horse archers that probably decided the outcome of the battle. On the other hand, it seems unlikely that the experienced indigenous scouts really did not know what the Russian army looked like. It seems still less probable that they did not realize the perils of attacking Alexander at Raven's Rock. It does seem reasonable to attribute the bishop's actions to a combination of desperation to prevent Alexander from invading Livonia, and crusader zeal. Certainly the Teutonic Knights were trained in the belief that God guided their swords. Then again, many of the German and Danish settlers would have been new to the frozen wildernesses of the Baltic with little if any combat experience in sub-zero conditions, though Bishop Hermann had been in Dorpat since 1224.

A peace settlement was negotiated which restored all the remaining crusader-held castles to Novgorod, including Izborsk. Almost immediately afterwards, the Livonian bishops and the Teutonic Knights had to deal with indigenous revolts in Prussia, Courland and Estonia, though these risings were due more to Mongol victories in Central Europe than to the Battle of Lake Peipus.

Thereafter the Church changed tack in its relations to the Russian Orthodox, using diplomacy rather than warfare to attempt to achieve a reunion with the Western Church. Pope Innocent IV (r. 1243–1254) was more concerned about the threat from the Golden Horde than the Rus and wrote to Prince Alexander in the hope of converting him to Catholicism and persuading him to join in a crusade against the Mongols. In another letter, the pope claims that Alexander actually made his submission to Rome, but this is doubtful, and the Russians make no reference to any such event.[47]

The Danes lost all interest in their Estonian colony and turned their attention to their possessions in Saxony. The Danish monarch devolved more and more of his authority to the Bishop of Reval (Tallinn) and finally the territory was sold to the Teutonic Order in 1346. The Swedes too lost their interest in Novgorod but not in the Finns, Karelians and other tribes on the borders of the principality, and by the end of the century they had succeeded in conquering southern Finland.

Alexander's terms for peace were generous, ensuring 20 years of relative harmony with the West. The victory at Lake Peipus had highlighted the weakness of Novgorod, and the *Veche* somewhat reluctantly conceded that it needed a prince residing permanently in the city. Under

---

[47] "The Religion of Russia" *Catholic Encyclopedia* Robert Appleton Company, New York 1917

Alexander the principality consolidated its hold over the north, expanded as far east as the Ural Mountains and beat off the raids of the pagan Lithuanians.

Alexander's attitude toward the Golden Horde was pragmatic. In 1246, its ruler Batu Khan sent word to him, stating that "you alone do not wish to subjugate yourself to me, to my power. But if you wish to preserve your land, come to me and see the glory of my realm."[48] Alexander duly journeyed to Batu's court at Saray and made his submission to the Horde. It was not difficult to convince his people that he had made the correct decision on their behalf, because the principality would not have survived a Mongol onslaught. Its towns and villages had been spared the devastation visited upon the rest of Russia, and its merchants could continue to grow rich.

In the following year, Alexander journeyed much further afield to the court of the Great Khan in Karakorum, Mongolia, in the company of his brother Andrey. Their father Yaroslav had died and Andrey sought the *yarlik* (commission) to succeed him as Grand Prince of Vladimir-Suzdal and of all Rus. They returned triumphantly in 1248, Andrey with the crown of all Rus and Alexander having had an opportunity to ingratiate himself with the Mongols. Once in power, however, Andrey II was determined to assert his independence and

---

[48] Nicolle, p.85.

married the daughter of Prince Daniel of Galicia, who plotted against the Golden Horde and – perhaps worse as far as the Orthodox Church was concerned – made overtures to the Bishop of Rome. In 1249 Alexander and his uncle Svyatoslav went to Saray and accused Andrey of keeping a portion of the Horde's tribute for himself. It is possible that Alexander damned his brother because he wanted the crown of Russia for himself. But the career of the prince thus far does not suggest a man intent on power at any price. It is more likely he wished to spare the punishment that would be visited on Novgorod and the rest of Russia, for the Horde habitually dealt with even the suggestion of defiance with ruthless cruelty. As it happened, the khan's wrath was confined mostly to the principality of Pereslavl, and Andrey fled to Novgorod in 1252. Unsurprisingly, Alexander would not receive him and he moved on to Sweden.

The Mongols were impressed with Alexander, who not only refused to support his brother but suppressed anti-Mongol revolts in his dominions. In fact he was held in such high esteem that Batu Khan made him his adopted son. Batu's son Sartak received Alexander in 1252 and conferred the Grand Duchy of Vladimir-Suzdal upon him. He was now ruler of the all the Rus. The Horde even allowed him to receive his brother Andrey back into Vladimir, after a suitable act of submission to the khan.

Alexander Nevsky died at Gorodets in the Grand Duchy of Vladimir on November 12, 1263, after a visit to Khan Berke. He was laid to rest in the Church of the Nativity of the Holy Mother of God in Vladimir. The Second Pskovian Chronicle described his passing:

> "Returning from the Golden Horde, the Great Prince Alexander, reached the city of Nizhny Novgorod, and remained there for several days in good health, but when he reached the city of Gorodets he fell ill ...

> "Great Prince Alexander, who was always firm in his faith in God, gave up this worldly kingdom ... And then he gave up his soul to God and died in peace on 12 November [1263], on the day when the Holy Apostle Philip is remembered ...

> "At this burial Metropolitan Archbishop Cyril said, "My children, you should know that the sun of the Suzdalian land has set. There will never be another prince like him in the Suzdalian land."

> "And the priests and deacons and monks, the poor and the wealthy, and all the people said: 'It is our end.'"[49]

In fact, it was not the end. A period of civil unrest

---

[49] Begunov, K., translator, *Second Pskovian Chronicle*, ("Isbornik," Moscow, 1955) pp.11–15.

followed Alexander's death, but the Grand Duchy survived, albeit under Tartar (Turco-Mongol) domination, and its resilience was due in no small part to Alexander Nevsky. While it is impossible to suppose that Alexander was unmoved at all by personal ambition, it seems that he was truly concerned for the welfare of Russia and its people. His submission to the Golden Horde spared Russia when other princes such as his brother Andrey were prepared to subject it to further misery. He rebuilt devastated infrastructure and strengthened the Orthodox Church, which was (and is) the pivotal focus of Russian unity, thus preparing the ground for the time in the 16th century when the Russian people could throw off the Tartar yoke. Not long after his death, the legend of Alexander the great warrior-saint and protector of Russia began. He was canonized by the Orthodox Church and to this day he is widely regarded as the most significant individual in Russian history.[50] The author of the *Life of Alexander Nevsky*, written in the 16th century, portrayed him in almost god-like terms:

> "This most Orthodox and noble Grand Prince Aleksandr Iaroslavich, greatly adorned by God, and worthy of praise; who was in the eighth generation from the sovereign Tsar and Grand Prince, Vladimir Sviatoslavich, Equal to the

[50] "Stalin voted third-best Russian," *BBC News* http://news.bbc.co.uk/2/hi/europe/7802485.stm.

Apostles, that had enlightened the land of Rus by holy baptism, and in the eleventh generation from Riurik; did earn by his virtues high and honorable praise not only from men but even from God himself….Though invested by God with the dignity of an earthly ruler, and having a wife, and being father of children, he nevertheless achieved greater lowly wisdom than any man. And he was very tall of stature, and his face was as beautiful to look at as that of Joseph the Fair. And his strength was such as if the strength of Samson had passed on to him. And his voice could be heard in the assembly like a trumpet.

"And his valor was equal to that of the Roman king Vespasian, son of Nero, who captured the whole land of Judaea, and arrayed his troops and commanded them to begin an assault on the town of Antipata; and the citizens, making a sally, destroyed his troops; but he came forth, and single-handed drove their force back to the city gate and said to his men, laughing: 'Wherefore did you leave me alone?' So, too, this Grand Prince Aleksander Iaroslavich; always a victor, and himself never defeated."[51]

The liturgy of the Russian Orthodox Church is even

---

[51] "Life of Alexander Nevsky," http://www.goldschp.net/SIG/nevskii/nev1.html.

more apotheotic, praising him as a wonder worker and the protector of all Russians.

> "Christ revealed you, O Blessed Alexander
>
> As a new and glorious worker of wonders;
>
> A man and a prince well pleasing to God
>
> And a divine treasure of the Russian Land.
>
> Today we assemble in faith and love
>
> To glorify the Lord by joyously remembering you.
>
> He granted you the grace of healing,
>
> Therefore entreat Him to strengthen your suffering spiritual children,
>
> And to save all Orthodox Christians."[52]

The Aftermath for the Teutonic Knights

For the Teutonic Order and the German bishops the Battle on the Ice had both negative and positive consequences. The Catholic Church, opting for negotiation with the Rus rather than their violent conversion, effectively abandoned the crusade in the North. Pope Innocent IV's successor Alexander IV continued his predecessor's policy of directing crusaders

---

[52] Troparion for the Repose of Alexander Nevsky https://www.oca.org/saints/troparia/2019/11/23.

against the Golden Horde and this required the good will of the Rus. This meant that the Germans could no longer invade Novgorod, though there were the occasional raids and border skirmishes. On the other hand peace with Novgorod meant that the Livonian bishops and Teutonic Knights could devote their energies to the serious revolts in Prussia, Courland, Semigallia and Livland which did not finally end until 1290. They were also involved in a struggle against the heathen Lithuanian tribes and this preoccupied them for the next 150 years or more.

All crusader states failed, and the Teutonic state was no exception. The Catholic states of the Middle East eventually succumbed to the Muslim reconquest for the simple reason that the crusading fervor upon which they depended wavered here and there over time. A united Christendom gave way to self-interested nations, and the same happened in the north. Without the full support and protection of Rome, the tide of German adventurers gradually ebbed and stagnated. The Order began to behave more pragmatically, granting more and more autonomy to the vassals as the number of its members diminished. It acted like any other state obsessed with maintaining its position against powerful neighbors – the Catholic Kingdom of Poland and the heathen Grand Duchy of Lithuania. In the late fourteenth century Lithuania converted to Catholicism and entered into personal union with Poland, thus presenting a united threat to the Knights. In 1410 Poland and Lithuania dealt a crippling blow to the Order at the Battle of Grunwald. Thereafter it fell into an irreversible decline, and the once great bastion of Catholicism ended its days by secularizing and converting to Protestantism in 1525. The foundations of the Order remained in the Holy Roman Empire and elsewhere, and the Teutonic Order has survived to this day, but it has reverted to its original mission: the care of the sick and the poor.

Ironically, Russia ceased to become a threat to the Ordenstaat after 1242. It has already been observed that Prince Alexander did not want to conquer Livonia, but this might seem surprising in the light of Russia's future obsession with gaining a seaport on the Baltic. The trade from the Black Sea passed to Ladoga, then along the Neva to the Baltic, but the Rus did not actually possess a strong fortified port at the mouth of the river. If Novgorod had conquered Tallinn or Riga, it would have gained such a port, but the principality's preoccupation was with the Neva and defending it against the Swedes, who continued to maintain an interest in Finland. Seven years after Lake Peipus, Sweden launched another crusade against the Finnish tribes which brought them into conflict with Novgorod. They built fortresses along the Novgorod borders and, provocatively, at the mouth of the Neva. The

1323 Treaty of Noteborg ended the long conflict and guaranteed Novgorod's access to the Baltic via the Neva.

The conflict between Sweden and Novgorod did not end, however, continuing through the next several centuries and culminating in the Ingrian War (1610–1617), which gave Ingria to Sweden and cut Russia off from the Baltic for more than a century. Russia's access to the Baltic was finally secured when Tsar Peter the Great laid the foundations of Saint Petersburg in the marshes of the Neva estuary in 1703.

Thus, the reason that Russia and the German Baltic territories did not clash again after 1242 was that both had more pressing issues. The Battle of Lake Peipus checked the German advance east, and both sides were content to let it decide the matter permanently.

The Legacy of the Battle

While Alexander has been a national hero in Russia for centuries, the Battle on the Ice was considered little more than a footnote in the annals of history until the rise of nationalism in the 19th century, when nations began concocting nation-building myths. In fact, the *Chronicle of Novgorod*, completed in 1471, devotes only one paragraph to the battle: "And the Knyaz [Prince Alexander] turned back to the lake and the Nemtsy and Chud [Estonians] men went after them. Seeing this,

Knyaz Olexander and all the men of Novgorod drew up their forces by Lake Chud at Uzmen by the Raven's rock; and the Nemtsy and Chud men rode at them driving themselves like a wedge through their army; and there was a great slaughter of Nemtsy and Chud men. And God and St. Sophia and the Holy Martyrs Boris and Gleb, for whose sake the men of Novgorod shed their blood, by the great prayers of those Saints, God helped Knyaz Alexander. And the Nemtsy fell there and the Chud men gave shoulder, and pursuing them fought with them on the ice, seven versts short of the Subol shore.2 And there fell of the Chud men a countless number; and of the Nemtsy 400, and fifty they took with their hands and brought to Novgorod."[53]

Modern historians have no difficulty understanding how relatively insignificant the battle was. It did not break the Teutonic Order or the rule of the German bishops in Estonia and Livonia. It did not extend Novgorod's borders, nor did it particularly boost Alexander. The immediate and most notable consequence was that it drew a border between the West and Russia that has endured in the Baltic to this day. Even then, however, the stability of that border was not due to the Battle of Lake Peipus itself but rather to weaknesses within the Teutonic Order.

In other words, the significance of the conflict was not

---

[53] Robert Michell & Neville Forbes (Trans.) *The Chronicle of Novgorod* Camden Society, London 1914.

its impact on history, but its symbolism. For Russians, the Battle of Lake Peipus halted the advance of the alien West, which threatened to destroy the Russian nation and Church. Alexander Nevsky became a great national hero as a defender of the monarchy and the Church until the Russian Revolution in 1917.[54] Despite the Soviets' disdain for the Church, Eisenstein's film made him a hero of the people ahead of World War II, substituting the fear of Catholicism with that of Nazi Germany.

Of course, both images conveniently ignore history. During Alexander's time, Russia was not a unified nation but a divided one subject to the Mongols; Alexander fought for a republic, not a monarchy, and he did not fight for the people but for the interest of the boyar and mercantile elite. Nonetheless, modern nations pay little attention to these facts when producing a national mythology.

In the West, the Battle on the Ice has also served as a powerful symbol. For the German Empire (1871–1918) and the Third Reich, the Knights represented a virtuous Teutonic civilization advancing to tame the Slavic brutes and take its right place in the world. Under the Nazis, *Lebensraum,* the plan to colonize the lands of the Slavs, was a core goal, but this was preceded by the unrealized

[54] Beatrice Heuser, Athena S. Leoussi (2018) *Famous Battles and How They Shaped the Modern World 1200 BCE–1302 AD: From Troy to Courtrai,* Pen and Sword.

Septemberprogramm of 1914, whereby Slavs and Jews in the east were to be removed and replaced by German settlers.[55] In this place, the former lands of the Livonian knights – Latvia and Estonia – were to be recolonized, and in 1918 the German population in the region offered Kaiser Wilhelm II the title Duke of Courland and Semigallia.

The German disdain for the Slavic east was expressed as far back as the 18th century when King Frederick the Great of Prussia annexed parts of Poland. He replaced the native population with German settlers, describing those he replaced as "slovenly Polish trash."[56] In a worldview where German civilization was the height of industrial, scientific, and cultural perfection, the Battle on the Ice was a symbol of Slavic brutality and perfidy.

Today the rhetoric of living space, German superiority, and Slavic barbarianism has almost entirely vanished, but shades of antagonism between Russia and Germany can still be found. To a large degree, the relationship between Germany and Russia has had a massive influence over European politics for centuries. In the 18th century, Russia and Prussia were asserting themselves as European

---

[55] Carsten, F.L. Review of *Griff nach der Weltmacht*, pp.751–753, in the *English Historical Review*, volume 78, Issue No. 309, October 1963, pp.752–753.

[56] "In fact, from Hitler to Hans Frank, we find frequent references to Slavs and Jews as 'Indians.' This, too, was a long standing trope. It can be traced back to Frederick the Great, who likened the 'slovenly Polish trash' in newly reconquered West Prussia to Iroquois." *Localism, Landscape, and the Ambiguities of Place: German-speaking Central Europe, 1860–1930* David Blackbourn, James N. Retallack University of Toronto 2007.

powers at the same time, and as the former became the dominant force in Eastern Europe, Prussia did so in Central Europe. Germany is now a leading power in the European Union and NATO, and Russia frequently views German interventions as attempts to push back its political and economic borders.[57] Latvia and Estonia remain two places where their respective interests clash.[58]

As this indicates, the ghosts of history – especially European history – are never really laid to rest.

Online Resources

Other books about medieval history by Charles River Editors

Other books about Russian history by Charles River Editors

Other books about the Battle on the Ice on Amazon

Further Reading

Basil Dmytryshyn, Medieval Russia 900–1700. New York: Holt, Rinehart and Winston, 1973.

John France, Western Warfare in the Age of the

---

[57] Dmitri Trenin (June 6, 2018) "Russia and Germany: From Estranged Partners to Good Neighbours," *Carnegie Moscow Center* https://carnegie.ru/2018/06/06/russia-and-germany-from-estranged-partners-to-good-neighbors-pub-76540.

[58] Ibid.

Crusades 1000–1300. Ithaca, NY: Cornell University Press, 1999.

Donald Ostrowski, "Alexander Nevskii's 'Battle on the Ice': The Creation of a Legend," Russian History/Histoire Russe, 33 (2006): 289–312.

Terrence Wise, The Knights of Christ. London: Osprey Publishing, 1984.

Dittmar Dahlmann Der russische Sieg über die „teutonischen Ritter" auf dem Peipussee 1242. In: Gerd Krumeich, Susanne Brandt (ed.): Schlachtenmythen. Ereignis–Erzählung–Erinnerung. Böhlau, Köln/Wien 2003, ISBN 3-41208-703-3, pp. 63–75. (in German)

Livländische Reimchronik. Mit Anmerkungen, Namenverzeichnis und Glossar. Ed. Leo Meyer. Paderborn 1876 (Reprint: Hildesheim 1963). (in German)

Anti Selart. Livland und die Rus' im 13. Jahrhundert. Böhlau, Köln/Wien 2012, ISBN 978-3-41216-006-7. (in German)

Anti Selart. Livonia, Rus' and the Baltic Crusades in the Thirteenth Century. Brill, Leiden/Boston, 2015.

Kaldalu, Meelis; Toots, Timo, Looking for the Border Island. Tartu: Damtan Publishing, 2005. Contemporary journalistic narrative about an Estonian youth attempting to uncover the secret of the Ice Battle. Accessible at https://web.archive.org/web/20110720125048/http://www.isamaa.ee/zona (password: ma_armastan_sind)

Joseph Brassey, Cooper Moo, Mark Teppo, Angus Trim, "Katabasis (The Mongoliad Cycle Book 4)" 47 North, 2013 ISBN 1477848215

David Savignac, The Pskov 3rd Chronicle, entries under the years 1240-1242,

Free Books by Charles River Editors

We have brand new titles available for free most days of the week. To see which of our titles are currently free, click on this link.

Discounted Books by Charles River Editors

We have titles at a discount price of just 99 cents everyday. To see which of our titles are currently 99 cents, click on this link.